COOKIE JARS

Ermagene Westfall

COLLECTOR BOOKS
A Division of Schroeder Publishing Co., Inc.

The current values in this book should be used only as a guide. They are not intended to set prices, which vary from one section of the country to another. Auction prices as well as dealer prices vary greatly and are affected by condition as well as demand. Neither the Author nor the Publisher assumes responsibility for any losses that might be incurred as a result of consulting this guide.

Printed by IMAGE GRAPHICS, INC., Paducah, Kentucky

DEDICATION

First, I want to dedicate this book to my family--my husband, Earl Ray, and our four children, Dirinda, Geoffrey, Brock, and Chantel. They have walked around jars on the floor, moved them to and from the kitchen table, kitchen counter top and even the bed on occasion until more shelves were built to display them properly.

Secondly, I dedicate this to the many cookie jar collectors everywhere, and hope you enjoy leafing through the pages as much as we have enjoyed collecting the jars you will see here.

ACKNOWLEDGEMENTS

I want to take this opportunity to give a special thanks to the following collectors who so trustingly loaned us jars to bring to our home and keep as long as needed to photograph. Sandy and Danny Brooks are remodeling their home and had most of their jars packed. Sandy, thanks so very much for going through box after box finding the jars I wanted to borrow.

Evlyn and Ralph Wolf have became dear friends to us. We met them at an antiques and collectibles show. Evlyn was also scouting for cookie jars. Ralph has a museum of agriculture. When we first met and began visiting, I thought the museum was Ralph's and the cookie jar collection Evlyn's, but I consider Ralph a cookie jar enthusiast too. Thanks to both of you.

John Washington doesn't collect cookie jars but has a tremendous collection of cut glass and the most unusual and beautiful pieces I have ever seen in my entire life. However, I borrowed his only jar, and he said it sat in the center of his stove for at least 35 or 40 years. That's what I call real friendship and trust. Thanks John.

Kay Hewitt was nice enough to let me borrow her jars and then re-borrow two of them again. Kay, thanks for letting me bug you twice.

Then last but not least, I would like to thank a great pair, my sister-in-law and brother-in-law, Evelyn and Richard Tuggle. Evelyn called long distance to find out for sure which jars I wanted to borrow. Then they packed them and brought them to us driving 100 miles one way. Evelyn is my husband's sister, and we four sometimes go on cookie jar excursions together, always having fun.

Again THANKS to each and every one of you and I sincerely hope the photos we have taken of your jars do them justice and meet with your greatest approval.

PREFACE

I had been collecting cookie jars for several years without really thinking of myself as a collector. I was looking for two particular jars which I finally found two years ago, and, in my search for them, I have bought many jars that several years ago I never would have dreamed of wanting or much less owning. I now display them with much pride.

My husband finally asked if I cared if he joined in my collection or if he should start one of his own. So now *we* have a cookie jar collection, and it has grown in leaps and bounds since our jar partnership. Our four children, Dirinda, 23; Geoffrey, 21; Brock, 19; and our youngest daughter, Chantel, 8; are very much interested in our collection and have given several jars to us as gifts on various occasions. They too are always "on the lookout" to help find jars we don't have.

Cookie jars have become a nationwide collectible almost overnight it seems. The price of cookie jars, as any other collectible, is based on availability. I also think prices vary considerably across the states.

While going to antiques and collectibles shows, flea markets and etc., I have found we are not the only cookie jar collectors by far. We now know of seven within a 100 mile radius of us. For this reason and because so many have asked why I didn't do a book, I have decided to write this one.

Several of the companies represented in this book are no longer in business, and so many of them in business only for a short period of time. Some of the companies listed did not make their own jars. Several different companies made jars for Walt Disney Productions; some were even made in Japan. I have put them into the catagory for whom they were made. Keep in mind that some of the molds were used by different companies. I have one jar in particuliar that I have seen made by at least three different companies.

I have listed markings to wording only. Prices listed are either what I have paid for jars or seen on them. Any mistakes, should they arise, in identifying any specific jars in this book are un-intentional. These jars have been sold to me as such or believed to be such by myself and other collectors.

We have taken the photographs of the jars ourselves and have tried our very best to get the truest colors possible. We also made the photos as big as we could so you can see more of the details.

Listed in this book is an unknown section. When I say "unknown" I am speaking primarily for myself and other collectors and dealers with whom I correspond. I would appreciate any knowledgeable letters concerning jars in this section.

I have compiled the knowledge I have gained from books, articles, antique dealers and other collectors as well as the knowledge acquired just by handling the jars themselves as to weight, color, glazes and etc. into a book that I hope might help to enlighten you in your collecting.

Abingdon; Special; I call this Granny. Both the top and bottom of this jar is marked; Mark: Top has incised "471"; bottom has incised "561", also stamped "Abingdon USA". $80.00-85.00.   Abingdon; Black Little Old Lady; Mark: incised "471". $150.00-175.00.

Abingdon; Hobby Horse; Mark: "Abingdon USA". $75.00-80.00.   Abingdon; Hippo; Mark: incised "549". $85.00-90.00.

Abingdon; Train; Mark: incised "651". $65.00-68.00. Abingdon; Three Bears; No mark. $48.00-55.00. (Also available with Abingdon mark.)

Abingdon; Humpty Dumpty; yellow brick wall; Mark: incised "663". $100.00-110.00. Regal China; Humpty Dumpty; gold trim, red brick wall; Mark: incised "Humpty Dumpty" "707". $115.00-135.00.

Abingdon; Clock; Mark: "Abingdon USA". $42.00-48.00.   Abingdon; Jack-in-Box; Mark: incised "611". $115.00-125.00.

Abingdon; Money Sack; yellow, gold trim; Mark: incised "558". $60.00-65.00.   Abingdon; Money Sack; White; Mark: incised "588". $50.00-55.00.

Abingdon; Little Miss Muffet; Mark: incised "662". $110.00-115.00. Regal China; Little Miss Muffet; flowers and gold trim; Mark: incised "Little Miss Muffet"; "705". $115.00-125.00.

Abingdon; Mother Goose; Mark: incised "695". $150.00-175.00. Abingdon; Little Bo-Peep; Mark: incised "694". $125.00-135.00.

Abingdon; Daisy; Mark: incised "667". $40.00-45.00.   Abingdon; Pineapple; Mark: incised "664". $55.00-60.00.

Alladin Plastic; Paddys Pig; cream; Unmarked. $15.00-18.00.   Alladin Plastic; Paddys Pig; blue; Unmarked. $15.00-18.00.

Ludowici Celadon; Dutch Girl; Unmarked. $20.00-25.00.   Ludowici Celadon;
Dutch Boy; Unmarked. $25.00-30.00.

American Bisque; Ring Cookies; Mark: "USA". $8.00-12.00.   American Bisque;
Pig; Mark: "Design Patent" (unreadable number) "A B Co". $25.00-28.00.

American Bisque; Cow; Mark: "Design Patent Applied A B Co". $25.00-28.00. American Bisque; Lamb; Mark: "Design Patent Applied A B Co". $30.00-35.00.

American Bisque; Apple; Mark: "USA". $15.00-18.00. American Bisque; Clown; Mark: "Design Patent 17119". $27.00-32.00.

American Bisque; Dutch Girl; fired in color. Mark: "USA". $38.00-42.00. American Bisque; Candy Baby; Unmarked. $35.00-37.00.

American Bisque; Boy Baby Elephant; Unmarked. $38.00-42.00. American Bisque; Girl Baby Elephant; Unmarked. $38.00-42.00.

American Bisque; Martha and George; Mark: "USA". $14.00-16.00.   American Bisque: Rabbit in Hat; Mark: "USA". $40.00-44.00.

American Bisque; Buck Lamb; Mark: "USA". $38.00-45.00.   American Bisque; Girl Lamb; Mark: "USA". $35.00-38.00.

American Bisque; Sitting Horse; Mark: "USA". $60.00-65.00. American Bisque; Donkey with Milk Wagon; Mark: "USA 740". $58.00-65.00.

American Bisque; Granny; Mark: "USA". $40.00-45.00. American Bisque; Sandman Cookies; Flasher Face; Mark: "801 USA". $48.00-52.00.

Regal China; Churn Boy; Unmarked. $70.00-75.00.   American Bisque; Umbrella Kids; Mark: "USA 739". $55.00-60.00.

American Bisque; Chef; Unmarked. $28.00-32.00.   American Bisque; Merry-Go-Round; Mark: "USA". $25.00-28.00.

American Bisque; Cat on Beehive; Mark: "USA". $30.00-32.00. American Bisque; Kittens with Ball of Yarn; Mark: "USA". $30.00-35.00.

American Bisque; Ring for Cookies; Mark: "USA". $20.00-22.00. American Bisque; Black Heating Stove; Mark: "USA". $15.00-18.00.

American Bisque; Blackboard Clown; Mark: "USA". $50.00-55.00.   American Bisque; Blackboard Bum; Mark: "USA". $50.00-55.00.

American Bisque; Blackboard School Boy; Mark: "USA". $55.00-60.00. American Bisque; Blackboard Little Girl; Mark: "USA". $55.00-60.00.

American Bisque; Churn; Mark: "USA". $12.00-15.00.   American Bisque; Clock; Unmarked. $22.00-25.00.

American Bisque; Cheerleaders; Flasher Face; Mark: "802 USA Corner Cookie Jar". $55.00-60.00.   American Bisque; After School Cookies; Mark: "USA 741". $25.00-28.00.

American Bisque; Boy Pig; Unmarked. $35.00-40.00.   American Bisque; Lady Pig; Unmarked. $35.00-40.00.

Regal China; Baby Pig; Mark: "404". $70.00-75.00.   American Bisque; Pig in the Polk; Mark: "USA". $38.00-42.00.

American Bisque; Cookie Truck; Mark: "USA". $38.00-42.00. American Bisque; Train; Unmarked. $22.00-25.00.

American Bisque; Rooster; Unmarked. $28.00-30.00. American Bisque; Animal Cookies; Mark: "USA". $18.00-22.00.

American Bisque; Yarn Doll; Unmarked. $45.00-48.00.   American Bisque; Cookie Barrel; Mark: "USA". $10.00-12.00.

American Bisque; Sad Iron; Mark: "USA". $38.00-42.00.   American Bisque; Majorette; Unmarked. $45.00-48.00.

American Bisque; Recipe Jar; Mark: "USA". $40.00-45.00.   American Bisque; Pinecones Coffee Pot; Mark: "USA". $18.00-25.00.

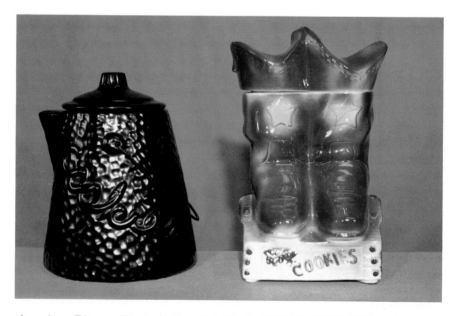

American Bisque; Black Coffee Pot; Mark: "USA". $10.00-12.00.   American Bisque; Boots; Mark: "USA 742". $60.00-65.00.

American Bisque; Cup of Chocolate; Mark: "USA". $25.00-28.00. American Bisque; Cup and Cookies Coffee Pot; Mark: "USA". $15.00-18.00.

American Bisque; Puppy in Blue Pot; Unmarked. $25.00-30.00. American Bisque; Puppy in Yellow Pot; Unmarked. $25.00-30.00.

American Bisque; Collegiate Owl; Mark: "USA". $28.00-35.00. American Bisque; Wooden Soldier; Mark: "USA". $42.00-45.00.

American Bisque; Yellow Chick; Unmarked. $30.00-35.00. American Bisque; White Chick; Mark: "USA". $38.00-42.00.

American Bisque; Jack in the Box; Mark: "USA". $38.00-42.00. American Bisque; Clown on Stage; Flasher Face; Mark: "805-USA". $35.00-40.00.

American Bisque; Bear; eyes open; Unmarked. $25.00-28.00. American Bisque; Bear; eyes closed, painted indented dots; Mark: "USA 130A". $32.00-36.00.

American Bisque; Pig; painted indented dots; Mark: "USA 128 A". $35.00-40.00. American Bisque; Cat; painted indented dots; Mark: "USA 131 A". $35.00-40.00.

American Bisque; Clown; painted indented dots; Mark: "USA 126 A". $35.00-40.00. American Bisque; Chick; painted indented dots; Mark: "USA 127 A". $35.00-40.00.

American Bisque; Clown; Mark: "USA". $28.00-32.00. American Bisque;
Elephant; Mark: "USA". $35.00-38.00.

American Bisque; Poodle; Mark: "USA". $38.00-42.00. American Bisque; Cat;
Unmarked. $32.00-35.00.

American Bisque; Snacks; Mark: "USA". $10.00-12.00.   American Bisque; Bear with Cookie; Unmarked. $38.00-42.00.

American Bisque; Pig with Patch on Pants; Mark: "USA". $42.00-48.00. American Bisque; Rooster; Unmarked. $25.00-30.00.

American Bisque; Farmer Pig; Mark: "USA". $42.00-45.00.   American Bisque; Seal on Igloo; Mark: "USA". $62.00-65.00.

American Bisque; Spaceship; Mark: "USA". $50.00-55.00.   American Bisque; Rabbit with Patches on Clothes; Mark: "USA". $45.00-48.00.

Belmont; Lion; Mark: "Belmont". $30.00-32.00.   Brayton; Large Mammy; Mark: "5 Brayton". $175.00-190.00.

Brush; Lantern; Mark: "K 1 Brush USA". $45.00-48.00.   Brush; Brown Cow; Mark: "Brush USA W 10". $60.00-65.00.

Brush; Little Boy Blue; Mark: "K 25 USA". $115.00-125.00. Brush; House; Mark: "W 31 Brush USA". $40.00-45.00.

Brush; Humpty Dumpty with Beanie; Mark: "Brush W 18". $75.00-80.00. Brush: Humpty Dumpty with Cowboy Hat; Mark: "W 29 Brush USA". $70.00-75.00.

Brush; Panda Bear; Mark: "W 21 Brush USA". $85.00-90.00.   Brush; Praying
Girl; Mark: "K 26 USA". $38.00-42.00.

Brush; Tulips; Mark: "137 USA". $25.00-28.00. Brush; Hen on Nest;
Unmarked. $28.00-32.00.

Brush; Treasure Chest; Mark: "W 28 Brush USA". $65.00-70.00.   Brush; Chick on Nest; Mark: "W 38 Brush USA". $85.00-90.00.

Brush; Granny; Mark: "W 19 Brush USA". $72.00-78.00.   Brush; Old Womans Shoe; Mark: "Brush W 23 USA". $68.00-75.00.

Brush; Clock; Mark: "W 20 Brush USA". $58.00-62.00.   Brush; Little Girl; Mark: "017 USA Brush". $95.00-100.00.

Brush; Grey Bunny; Mark: "W 25 Brush USA". $62.00-68.00.   Brush; White Bunny; Mark: "W 25 Brush USA". $58.00-65.00.

Brush; Teddy Bear; feet apart; Mark: "W 14". $58.00-62.00.   Brush; Teddy Bear; feet together; Mark: "014 USA". $45.00-50.00.

Brush; Davy Crockett; Mark: "USA". $110.00-120.00.   Brush; Puppy Police; Mark: "W 39 Brush USA". $90.00-95.00.

Brush; Three Bears; Mark: "K 2 Brush USA". $32.00-35.00.   Brush; Covered Wagon; Mark: "W 30 Brush USA". $160.00-180.00.

Brush; Donkey with Cart; ears down; Mark: "W 33 Brush USA". $100.00-110.00.   Brush; Formal Pig; Mark: "W 7 USA". $70.00-75.00.

Brush; Happy Squirrel; Mark: "W 15 USA". $55.00-58.00.   Brush; Squirrel on Log; Mark: "USA". $45.00-50.00.

Brush; Peter Peter Pumpkin Eater; Mark: "W 24 USA". $98.00-105.00.   Brush; Cinderella's Pumpkin; Mark: "W 32 Brush USA". $75.00-78.00.

Brush; Clown; Mark: "W 22 Brush USA". $65.00-68.00.   Brush; Circus Horse; Unmarked. $125.00-140.00.

Brush; Elephant with Ice Cream Cone; blue coat; Mark: "W 8 USA". $80.00-85.00.   Brush; Elephant with Ice Cream Cone; yellow coat; Mark: "W 8 Brush USA". $80.00-85.00.

Brush; Little Red Riding Hood; Mark: "Brush K 24 USA". $110.00-115.00. Brush; Dog with Basket; Unmarked. $48.00-52.00.

California Originals; Pelican; Unmarked. $35.00-40.00. California Originals; Brown Bear; Mark: "G-405". $25.00-30.00.

California Originals; Rabbit; Unmarked. $20.00-25.00.   California Originals; Elfs School House; Unmarked. $32.00-35.00.

California Originals; Ernie; Mark: "Muppets Inc 973". $44.00-48.00.   California Originals; Cookie Monster; Mark : "Muppets Inc 970". $38.00-40.00.

California Originals; Count; Unmarked. $48.00-52.00. Roman Ceramics; Smokey Bear; Mark: (a "C" through a "W"), then "USA". $35.00-40.00.

Cardinal; Cookie Garage; Mark: "Cardinal USA". $38.00-42.00. Cardinal; Boys Head; Mark; "USA Cardinal". $48.00-52.00.

Cardinal; Soldier; Mark: "312 USA Cardinal". $48.00-50.00.   Cardinal; Round House; Mark: "Cardinal 3100 USA". $32.00-35.00.

Cardinal; French Chef; Mark: "Cardinal USA". $40.00-45.00.   Cardinal; Cookie Safe; Mark: "Cardinal 309 USA". $24.00-28.00.

Cardinal; Sack of Cookies; Mark: "USA #4260". $25.00-28.00.   Coors; Milk Can; Mark: "Coors". $32.00-38.00.

DeForrest of California; Cookie King; Mark: "DeForrest of Calif 1957". $40.00-45.00.   DeForrest of California; Clown; Mark: "DeForrest of Calif USA 5-24-57". $28.00-32.00.

Doranne of California; Cow Jumped over the Moon; Unmarked. $70.00-75.00. Doranne of California; Shoe; Unmarked. $22.00-25.00.

Doranne of California; Mother Goose; Mark: "C J 16 USA". $60.00-65.00. Doranne of California; Hen with Basket of Eggs; Mark: "C J 103 USA Doranne". $30.00-32.00.

Doranne of California; Duck with Corn; Mark: "C J 104 USA Doranne".
$30.00-32.00.   Doranne of California; Fire Plug; Mark: "C J 50". $30.00-35.00.

Doranne of California; Cow with Milk Can; Mark: "C J 106 USA DORANNE".
$30.00-32.00.   F. & F. Mold & Die Works; Aunt Jemima; Mark: "F&F Mold
& Die Works Dayton Ohio Made in USA". $130.00-140.00.

Frankoma; Brown & Beige; Word "Cookies" on handle. Mark: "Frankoma 25 F". $35.00-40.00.   Frankoma; Green & Grey Concave; Mark: "Frankoma 205". $25.00-28.00.

Frankoma; Black Barrel with Ears; Mark: "97 V Frankoma". $30.00-35.00.   Fredricksburg Art Pottery; Pink Dove; Mark: "FAPCO". $38.00-42.00.

Fredricksburg Art Pottery; Green Dove; Mark: "FAPCO". $38.00-42.00.
Fredricksburg Art Pottery; Blue Dove; Mark: "FAPCO". $38.00-42.00.

Fredricksburg Art Pottery; Brown Chicken with Little Chick on back; Mark:
"USA FAPCO". $25.00-28.00. Fredricksburg Art Pottery; Brown & Green
Chicken; Mark: "USA FAPCO". $30.00-35.00.

47

Fredricksburg Art Pottery; Windmill; red trim; Mark: "FAPCo". $35.00-38.00. Fredricksburg Art Pottery; Windmill; blue trim; Mark: "FAP-Co". $38.00-42.00.

Gilner; Rooster; Mark: "Gilner G 622". $28.00-32.00. Hall China; White and Gold; Mark: "Flare-Ware by Hall China Made in USA". $55.00-60.00.

Hall China; Poppy; Mark: "Hall's Superior Quality Kitchenware Made in USA". $60.00-75.00. Hall China; Autumn Leaf; Mark: "Hall's Superior Quality Kitchenware Tested and approved by Mary Dunbar Jewel Homemakers Institute". $120.00-130.00.

Hanna Barbera Productions; Yogi Bear; Mark: "Hanna Barbera Productions 1361 USA". $100.00-115.00. Harvey Productions Inc; Casper; Mark: "Harvey Productions Inc. USA ". $250.00-300.00.

Hull Pottery; Big Apple; Unmarked. $25.00-28.00.   Hull Pottery; Duck; Mark: "Hull 966 USA". $45.00-55.00.

Hull Pottery; Little Red Riding Hood; Mark: "967 Hull Ware Little Red Riding Hood Patent Applied For USA". $115.00-120.00.   Hull Pottery; Little Red Riding Hood; Mark: "Pat. Des. No. 135889 USA". $95.00-105.00.

Hull Pottery; Little Red Riding Hood; Mark: "967 Hull Ware Little Red Riding Hood Patent applied For USA". $95.00-105.00. Hull Pottery; Little Red Riding Hood; Mark: "967 Hull Ware Little Red Riding Hood Patent Applied For USA". $95.00-105.00.

Hull Pottery; Little Red Riding Hood; closed basket; Mark: "Pat. Des. No. 135889 USA". $90.00-100.00. Hull Pottery; Daisy; Mark: "Hull USA No. 48". $25.00-28.00.

Los Angeles Potteries; Cookies and Cookie Cutters; Mark: "60 Los Angeles Potteries XX98 Made in USA". $25.00-28.00.   Los Angeles Potteries; Cookies with Nut on Lid; Mark: "Los Angeles Potteries XX91". $18.00-22.00.

Los Angeles Potteries; Apple and Apple Blossoms; Mark: "Los Angeles Potteries 520". $12.00-15.00.   Maddux of California; Humpty Dumpty; Mark: "2113 Maddux of Calif. USA". $38.00-45.00.

Mar-Crest; Brown with Flowers and Dots; Mark: "Mar-Crest Oven Proof Stoneware USA". $22.00-25.00.   Maurice of California; Kittens in Shoe; Mark: "Maurice of Calif USA". $35.00-40.00.

Maurice of California; Love Me Puppy; Mark: "Maurice of Calif USA". $18.00-22.00.   Maurice of California; Love Me Puppy (gloss finish); Mark: "USA". $15.00-18.00.

Maurice of California; Rabbit; Mark: "Maurice of Calif. USA JD-17". $35.00-38.00. Maurice of California; Bear beating Drum; Mark: "Maurice of Calif.". $25.00-28.00.

Morton Potteries; Hen with Chicks; Unmarked. $50.00-55.00. Morton Potteries; Turkey with Little Turkey on Back; Unmarked. $65.00-68.00.

McCoy; Dark Indian; Mark: "McCoy USA". $160.00-175.00.   McCoy; Light Indian; Mark: "McCoy USA". $145.00-155.00.

McCoy; Tepee; Mark: "McCoy USA 137". $145.00-150.00.   McCoy; Honey Bear; Mark: "McCoy USA". $55.00-60.00.

McCoy; Log Cabin; Mark: "McCoy USA 136". $58.00-62.00.   McCoy; Davy
Crockett Head; Mark: "USA". $325.00-340.00.

McCoy; Circus Horse; Mark: "McCoy USA". $88.00-92.00.   McCoy; Barnums
Animals; Mark: "152 USA". $70.00-75.00.

McCoy; Clown Bust; Mark: "McCoy". $30.00-35.00.   McCoy; Animals Crackers; Mark: "McCoy USA". $30.00-35.00.

McCoy; Sad Clown; Mark: "255 McCoy USA". $30.00-35.00.   McCoy; Little Clown; Mark: "McCoy". $50.00-54.00.

McCoy

McCoy; Dutch Girl; Mark: "McCoy". $55.00-60.00.   McCoy; Dutch Boy; Mark: "McCoy". $30.00-32.00.

McCoy; Windmill; Mark: "McCoy USA". $55.00-62.00.   McCoy; Dutch Treat Barn; Unmarked. $25.00-28.00.

McCoy; Fat Pig; Mark: "201 McCoy USA". $35.00-38.00.   McCoy; Ear of Corn;
Mark: "McCoy USA". $90.00-95.00.

McCoy; Betsy Baker; Mark: "184 McCoy USA". $40.00-45.00.   McCoy; Bobby
Baker; Mark: "183 McCoy USA". $22.00-25.00.

McCoy; Black Cookstove; Mark: "McCoy USA". $28.00-35.00.   McCoy; White
Cookstove; Mark: "McCoy USA" (also just "USA"). $22.00-28.00.

McCoy; Chef Head; Mark: "McCoy USA". $55.00-58.00.   McCoy; Mammy with
Cauliflower; Mark: "McCoy USA". $450.00-500.00.

McCoy; Old Strawberry; Mark: "McCoy USA". $28.00-32.00.   McCoy; Pineapple; Mark: "McCoy USA". $30.00-35.00.

McCoy; Orange; Mark: "257 McCoy USA". $28.00-32.00.   McCoy; Lemon; Mark: "262 McCoy USA". $30.00-32.00.

McCoy; Red Apple; Unmarked. $25.00-28.00.   McCoy; Bunch of Bananas; Mark: "McCoy". $55.00-60.00.

McCoy; Christmas Tree; Mark: "McCoy USA". $250.00-275.00.   McCoy; Pinecones on Basketweave; Mark: "McCoy USA". $28.00-32.00.

McCoy; Raggedy Ann; Mark: "151 USA". $38.00-45.00.   McCoy; Fireplace; Mark: "USA". $55.00-62.00.

McCoy; Jack-O-Lantern; Mark: "McCoy USA". $200.00-225.00.   McCoy; Black Cat; Mark: "McCoy 207". $68.00-75.00.

McCoy

McCoy; Polar Bear; Unmarked. $65.00-68.00. McCoy; Polar Bear; Mark: "McCoy". $40.00-45.00.

McCoy; Brown Bear; Mark: "McCoy USA". $70.00-75.00. McCoy; Hamms Bear; Mark: "148 USA". $78.00-84.00.

McCoy; Snow Bear; Mark: "McCoy USA". $48.00-52.00.   McCoy; Upside Down Bear; Mark: "210 McCoy USA". $30.00-35.00.

McCoy; Kissing Penguins; Mark: "McCoy USA". $55.00-60.00.   McCoy; White Pel-guin; This bird has the stance of a penguin but the beak of a pelican. So what to call it--? Mark: "McCoy". $55.00-60.00.

McCoy; Green Pel-guin; Mark: "McCoy". $65.00-68.00.   McCoy; Yellow Pel-guin; Mark: "McCoy". $60.00-65.00.

McCoy; Chiffonier; Mark: "McCoy USA". $52.00-58.00.   McCoy; Rooster; Mark: "258 McCoy USA". $38.00-42.00.

McCoy; Frontier Family; Unmarked. $42.00-45.00.   McCoy; Frontier Family; reverse side.

McCoy; Cookie Safe; Mark: "USA". $30.00-35.00.   McCoy; Cookie Bank; Mark: "McCoy USA". $78.00-85.00.

McCoy; Cookie House; Mark: "McCoy USA". $68.00-75.00.   McCoy; Churn; Unmarked. $15.00-18.00.

McCoy; Black Train Engine; Mark: "McCoy USA". $70.00-75.00.   McCoy; Caboose; Mark: "McCoy USA". $75.00-80.00.

McCoy; Cookie Wagon; Mark: "McCoy USA". $58.00-62.00.   McCoy; Touring Car; Mark: "McCoy USA". $62.00-68.00.

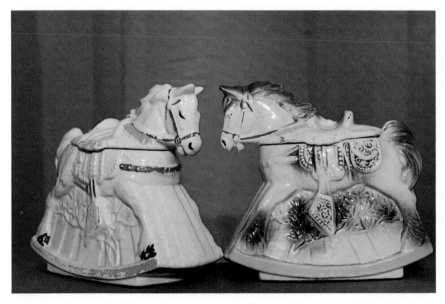

McCoy; Hobby Horse; white underglaze; Mark: "McCoy USA". $52.00-56.00.   McCoy; Hobby Horse; brown underglaze; Mark: "McCoy USA". $60.00-68.00.

McCoy; Mushrooms on Stump; Mark: "214 McCoy USA". $20.00-25.00.   McCoy; Rabbit on Stump; Mark: "McCoy USA". $20.00-25.00.

McCoy; Squirrel on Log; Mark: "USA". $20.00-25.00.   McCoy; Cookie Boy; yellow; Mark: "McCoy". $65.00-70.00.

McCoy; Monkey on Stump; Mark: "253 McCoy USA". $20.00-25.00. McCoy; Cookie Boy; white; Mark: "McCoy". $64.00-68.00.

McCoy; Burlap Bag; Mark: "158 USA". $18.00-22.00. McCoy; Burlap Bag with Redbird; Mark: "158 USA". $28.00-32.00.

McCoy

McCoy; Wren House; pink bird; Mark: "McCoy USA". $55.00-60.00.   McCoy;
Wren House; brown bird; Mark: "McCoy USA". $58.00-62.00

McCoy; Pears on Basketweave; Mark: "McCoy USA". $28.00-32.00.   McCoy;
Yellow Pear; Mark: "McCoy USA". $50.00-58.00.

McCoy; Foridden Fruit; Mark: "McCoy USA". $38.00-42.00. McCoy; New Strawberry; Mark: "McCoy 263 USA". $20.00-25.00.

McCoy; Apples on Basketweave; Mark: "McCoy USA". $28.00-32.00. McCoy; Yellow Apple; Mark: "McCoy USA". $25.00-30.00.

McCoy; Mouse on Clock; Unmarked. $20.00-25.00.   McCoy; Lollipops; Mark: "McCoy USA". $25.00-30.00.

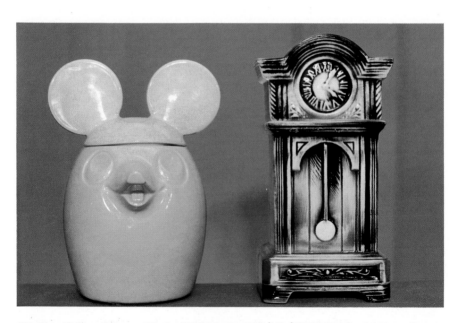

McCoy; Yellow Mouse; Mark: "200 McCoy USA". $15.00-18.00.   McCoy; Grandfather Clock; Mark: "USA". $50.00-55.00.

McCoy; Black Lantern; Mark: "McCoy USA". $38.00-40.00. McCoy; Fortune Cookies; Mark: "McCoy USA". $25.00-30.00.

McCoy; Granny; Mark: "USA". $45.00-48.00. McCoy; Mammy; Mark: "McCoy". $85.00-95.00.

McCoy; W.C. Fields Head; Mark: "153 USA". $98.00-105.00.   McCoy; Lamb
on Basketweave; Mark: "McCoy USA". $35.00-38.00.

McCoy; Monk; Unmarked. $25.00-28.00.   McCoy; Yellow Hobnail; Unmarked.
$20.00-25.00.

McCoy; Cylinder with Fruit; Mark: "McCoy USA". $15.00-18.00. McCoy; Cylinder with Vegetables; Mark: "McCoy USA". $15.00-18.00.

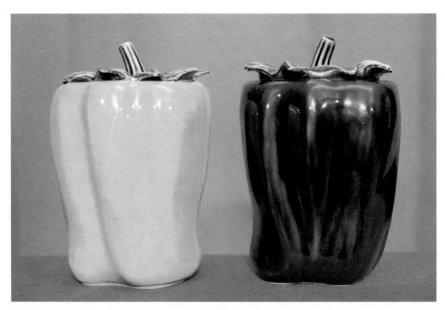

McCoy; Yellow Pepper; Mark: "157 McCoy USA". $15.00-18.00. McCoy; Green Pepper; Mark: "157 McCoy USA". $15.00-18.00.

McCoy; Wedding Jar; Mark: "McCoy USA". $55.00-58.00. McCoy; Coffee Grinder; Mark: "McCoy USA". $22.00-25.00.

McCoy; Bugs Bunny; Unmarked. $38.00-42.00. McCoy; Popeye; Mark: (ink stamped) "McCoy USA". $45.00-50.00.

McCoy; Yosemite Sam; Unmarked. $38.00-42.00.   McCoy; Bronze Milk Can; Mark: "USA". $25.00-28.00.

McCoy; Brown Cat on Coal Bucket; Mark: "219 McCoy USA". $35.00-38.00.   McCoy; Cat on Basketweave; Mark: "McCoy USA". $35.00-40.00.

McCoy; Three Little Kittens on Maroon Yarn; Mark: "McCoy USA".
$35.00-38.00. McCoy; Three Little Kittens on Yellow Yarn; Mark: "McCoy
USA". $32.00-35.00.

McCoy; Three Little Kittens on Green Yarn; Mark: "McCoy USA".
$32.00-35.00. McCoy; Two Kittens in Basket; Mark: "McCoy USA".
$185.00-200.00.

McCoy; Basket of Fruit; Mark: "McCoy USA". $48.00-52.00. McCoy; Picnic
Basket; Mark: "USA". $38.00-45.00.

McCoy; Cookie Pot; Mark: "McCoy USA". $28.00-30.00. McCoy; Coffee Mug;
Mark: "USA". $28.00-30.00.

McCoy; Gaytime Pitcher; plant small; Mark: "McCoy USA". $25.00-30.00.
McCoy; Gaytime Pitcher; plant grown; Mark: "McCoy USA". $25.00-30.00.

McCoy; Yellow Rooster; Mark: "McCoy USA". $50.00-55.00.   McCoy; Hen on Nest; Mark: "USA". $52.00-55.00.

McCoy; Grey Rooster; Mark: "McCoy USA". $55.00-60.00.   McCoy; Basket of Eggs; Mark: "0274 McCoy USA". $22.00-25.00.

McCoy; Duck with Leaf; Mark: "USA". $55.00-60.00.   McCoy; Turkey; Mark: "McCoy USA". $100.00-115.00.

McCoy; Tan Basketweave, American Eagle; Unmarked. $18.00-22.00. McCoy; Brown Basketweave, American Eagle; Unmarked. $22.00-25.00.

McCoy; Friendship 7, Spaceship; Unmarked. $60.00-68.00. McCoy; World Globe; Mark: "McCoy USA". $95.00-100.00.

McCoy; Astronauts; Mark: "USA". $70.00-75.00.   McCoy; Apollo; Mark: "260 McCoy USA". $175.00-190.00.

McCoy; Dog in Basket; Mark: "McCoy USA". $42.00-45.00.   McCoy; Snoopy on Dog House; Mark: "1970 United Feature Syndicate Inc. World Rights Reserved Made in USA". $90.00-105.00.

McCoy; Thinking Puppy; Mark: "0272 McCoy USA". $20.00-25.00. McCoy; Puppy Holding Sign; Mark: "McCoy USA". $48.00-52.00.

McCoy; Rocking Chair Dalmations; (Mother Dog with Eleven Pups in Chair); Mark: "McCoy USA". $135.00-140.00. McCoy; Mac Dog; Mark: "208 USA". $45.00-48.00.

McCoy; Sack of Cookies; Mark: "McCoy USA". $35.00-40.00. McCoy; Chipmunk; Mark: "McCoy USA". $70.00-75.00.

McCoy; Black Pot Bellied Stove; Mark: "McCoy USA". $25.00-28.00. McCoy; White Pot Bellied Stove; Mark: "McCoy USA" (also just "USA"). $28.00-32.00.

McCoy; Kangaroo with Yellow-Tan underglaze; Mark: "McCoy USA". $175.00-190.00. McCoy; Blue Kangaroo; Unmarked. $75.00-80.00.

McCoy; Elephant; Unmarked. $78.00-82.00. McCoy; Drum; Mark: "McCoy USA". $35.00-40.00.

McCoy; Mother Goose; brown underglaze; Mark: "McCoy USA".
$70.00-75.00.   McCoy; Mother Goose; white underglaze; Mark: "McCoy USA".
$65.00-70.00.

McCoy; Wishing Well; Mark: "McCoy USA". $28.00-32.00.   McCoy; Square,
with hand decoration; This one was once a rose; Mark: "McCoy". $15.00-20.00.

McCoy; Oaken Bucket; Mark: "USA". $12.00-15.00.   McCoy; Double Headed Duck; Each side of lid shows a duck head; Mark: "McCoy USA". $38.00-40.00.

McCoy; Asparagus; Unmarked. $25.00-30.00.   McCoy; Basket of Potatoes; Mark: "0274 McCoy USA". $28.00-32.00.

McCoy; White Cylinder with Chef Decal; Mark: "McCoy USA". $22.00-28.00. McCoy; White Cylinder with hand painted Apple; Mark: "McCoy USA". $18.00-22.00.

McCoy; Nabisco Jar; Mark: "McCoy 78 USA". $42.00-45.00. McCoy; White Cylinder with hand painted Wheat; Mark: "McCoy USA". $22.00-25.00.

McCoy; Mr. & Mrs. Owl; Mark: "McCoy USA". $55.00-58.00.   McCoy; Brown Owl; Mark: "204 McCoy USA". $22.00-25.00.

McCoy; Woodsy Owl; Mark: "USA". $75.00-80.00.   McCoy; Hocus Rabbit; Mark: "211 McCoy". $25.00-30.00.

McCoy; Cream colored Rabbit; Mark: "211 McCoy USA". $25.00-28.00.   McCoy; Timmy Tortoise; Mark: "271 McCoy USA". $25.00-28.00.

McCoy; Mary, Mary; Unmarked. $30.00-35.00.   McCoy; Little Bo-Peep; Unmarked. $30.00-35.00.

McCoy; Humpty Dumpty; Unmarked. $30.00-35.00.   McCoy; Little Miss Muffet; Unmarked. $30.00-35.00.

McCoy; Brown Barrel with Cookie Sign; Mark: "146 McCoy USA". $15.00-18.00.   McCoy; Black Barrel with Cookie Sign; Mark: "146 McCoy USA". $15.00-18.00.

McCoy; Tureen; Mark: "McCoy USA". $32.00-35.00.   McCoy; Tomato; Mark: "McCoy USA". $25.00-28.00.

McCoy; Gingerbread Man; Mark: "USA". $45.00-48.00.   McCoy; Kissin' Don't Last, Cookin' Do; Mark: "USA". $22.00-28.00.

McCoy; Small Brown Cookie Barrel; Mark: "USA". $12.00-15.00.   McCoy; Large Brown Cookie Barrel; Mark: "USA". $10.00-12.00.

McCoy; Clown in Yellow Barrel; Mark: "McCoy USA". $38.00-42.00.   McCoy; Clown in Blue Barrel; Mark: "McCoy USA". $38.00-42.00.

McCoy; Clown in Green Barrel; Mark: "McCoy USA". $38.00-42.00.   McCoy;
Pirates Chest; Mark: "252 McCoy USA". $45.00-50.00.

McCoy; White with Gold Trim; Mark: "USA". $28.00-35.00.   McCoy; Pitcher
with Blue Willow Decor; Mark: "202 McCoy USA". $35.00-40.00.

McCoy; Clyde Dog; Mark: "McCoy 182". $42.00-45.00.   McCoy; Animal Cracker Clown; This Clown does not have the raised dots like the one shown on page 57. Mark: "McCoy USA". $30.00-35.00.

McCoy; Basket of Strawberries; Unmarked. $28.00-32.00.   McCoy; Dog in Dog House; Unmarked. $42.00-45.00.

McCoy; Cookie Box; Mark: "USA". $55.00-60.00.   McCoy; Liberty Bell; Mark: "McCoy USA". $30.00-35.00.

McCoy; Football with Player; Mark: "222 McCoy USA". $30.00-35.00.   McCoy; Baseball with Player; Mark: "221 McCoy USA". $30.00-35.00.

McCoy; Basket of Tomatoes; Mark: "McCoy USA". $25.00-28.00. McCoy;
Koala Bear; Mark: "216 McCoy USA". $35.00-40.00.

National Silver; Mammy; Mark: "N.S.". $90.00-105.00. National Silver; Chef;
Mark: "N.S.". $90.00-100.00.

Napco; Bo-Peep; Mark: (Stamped) "J.C. Napco-1957 K 2292". $38.00-42.00. Pantry Parade; Tomato; Mark: "Pantry Parade Co. USA". $20.00-25.00.

Pan American Art; Clown; Mark: "Pan American Art". $38.00-42.00. Pan American Art; Southern Belle; Mark: "Pan American Art". $45.00-50.00.

Pearl China; Chef; Mark: "Pearl China Co. Hand Decorated 22 Kt. Gold USA" (also incised "639"). $175.00-200.00. Pearl China; Mammy; brown slave collar around neck; Mark: "Pearl China Co. Hand Decorated 22 Kt. Gold USA". $375.00-410.00.

Pee Dee Co.; Fruit Kids, Albert Apple; Mark: "F K R 1942 P D & Co Inc Albert Apple". $55.00-60.00. Pee Dee Co.; Fruit Kids, Stella Strawberry; Mark: "F K R 1942 P D & Co Inc Stella Strawberry". $60.00-65.00.

Pfaltzgraff Pottery Co.; Derby Dan; Mark: " 'Muggsy' The Pfaltzgraff Pottery Co York Penn Designed by Jessop". $50.00-55.00. Pillsbury Company; Pillsbury Doughboy; Mark: "The Pillsbury Company 1973". $42.00-48.00.

Poppytrail by Metlox; Bear; Mark: "Made in Poppytrail Calif". $30.00-38.00. Poppytrail by Metlox; Squirrel on Stump; Mark: "Made in USA". $25.00-28.00.

Poppytrail by Metlox; Rose; Mark: "Made in USA". $35.00-38.00.   Poppytrail by Metlox; Drum with Girl, Boy and Dog; Mark: "Made in Poppytrail Calif USA". $28.00-35.00.

Poppytrail by Metlox; Raggedy Andy; Mark: "Made in Poppytrail Calif". $32.00-38.00.   Poppytrail by Metlox; Raggedy Ann; Mark: "Made in Poppytrail Calif". $32.00-38.00.

Poppytrail by Metlox; The Bandit; Unmarked. $38.00-42.00. Poppytrail by Metlox; Mouse Mobile; Unmarked. $32.00-38.00.

Poppytrail by Metlox; Squirrel on Pinecone; Mark: "Made in USA". $20.00-25.00. Poppytrail by Metlox; Clown; Mark: "Made in Poppytrail Calif". $40.00-45.00.

Poppytrail by Metlox, Pottery Guild

Poppytrail by Metlox; Lamb Head; Unmarked. $22.00-28.00. Poppytrail by Metlox; Cat Head; Unmarked. $25.00-30.00.

Poppytrail by Metlox; Pig; Mark: "Made in Poppytrail Calif. USA". $28.00-32.00. Pottery Guild; Rooster; Mark: "Hand Painted Pottery Guild of America". $35.00-38.00.

Ransburg; Black Ball Shape; Mark: "Ransburg Genuine Hand Painted Indianapolis USA". $22.00-25.00. Red Wing; Aqua with Dutch People; Unmarked. $55.00-60.00.

Red Wing; Yellow Baker; Mark: Incised "Red Wing USA"; also stamped "Red Wing Pottery USA". $55.00-60.00. Red Wing; Yellow Dutch Girl; Mark: incised "Red Wing"; also stamped "Red Wing Pottery USA". $58.00-65.00.

Red Wing; Blue Baker; Mark: incised "Red Wing USA". $55.00-60.00.   Red Wing; Blue Dutch Girl; Mark: incised "Red Wing USA". $55.00-60.00.

Red Wing; Beige Baker; Mark: stamped "Red Wing Pottery". $55.00-60.00.   Red Wing; Beige Dutch Girl; Mark: incised "Red Wing"; also Stamped "Red Wing Pottery". $55.00-60.00.

Red Wing; Bob White; Unmarked. $65.00-70.00. Red Wing; Pineapple; Mark: incised "Red Wing". $40.00-45.00.

Red Wing; Beige Monk; Mark: "Red Wing Hand Painted" (stamped); incised "Red Wing USA". $55.00-60.00. Red Wing; Blue Monk; Mark: incised "Red Wing USA". $60.00-65.00.

Regal China, Robbinson Ransbottom Pottery

Regal China; Quaker Oats; (Oatmeal Cookie Recipe on Back); Mark: "Regal China". $80.00-85.00. Regal China; Davy Crockett Head; Mark: "Translucent Vitrified China C Miller 55-140 B". $85.00-90.00.

Robbinson Ransbottom Pottery; Oscar; Unmarked. $32.00-35.00. Robbinson Ransbottom Pottery; Girl Head; Wrong Lid; Unmarked. $35.00-38.00.

**Robbinson Ransbottom Pottery; Brownie; Mark: "Brownie" on collar; "USA".
$42.00-45.00. Robbinson Ransbottom Pottery; Firechief; Mark: "Firechief" on
collar; "USA". $42.00-45.00.**

**Robbinson Ransbottom Pottery; Captain; Mark: "Captain" on collar; "USA".
$42.00-45.00. Robbinson Ransbottom Pottery; Preacher; Mark: "Preacher" on
collar; "USA". $42.00-45.00.**

Robbinson Ransbottom Pottery; World War II Soldier; Unmarked. $58.00-62.00.   Robbinson Ransbottom Pottery; World War I Soldier; Unmarked. $58.00-62.00.

Robbinson Ransbottom Pottery; Brown Rooster; Mark: "R.R.P.Co. Roseville O. USA". $30.00-35.00.   Robbinson Ransbottom Pottery; Cream Colored with Aqua Rings; Mark: "R.R.P.Co. Roseville Ohio #350". $22.00-25.00.

Robbinson Ransbottom Pottery; Sheriff Pig; yellow hat; Mark: "R.R.P. Co. Roseville Ohio 363". $32.00-35.00.   Robbinson Ransbottom Pottery; Sheriff Pig; grey hat; Mark: "R.R.P. Co. Roseville Ohio 363". $32.00-35.00.

Robbinson Ransbottom Pottery; Peter, Peter, Pumpkin Eater; Mark: "USA R.R.P.Co Roseville Ohio 1502". $55.00-60.00.   Robbinson Ransbottom Pottery; Cow Jumped over the Moon; Mark: "R.R.P.Co. Roseville Ohio 1317". $38.00-42.00.

Robbinson Ransbottom Pottery; Jocko; (This is not Jocko's original hat); Mark: "R.R.P.Co. USA Roseville O". $68.00-72.00. Robinson Ransbottom Pottery; Wise Bird; Mark: "R.R.P.Co Roseville O 359". $25.00-28.00.

Robbinson Ransbottom Pottery; Snowman; Mark: "R.R.P.Co USA Roseville O". $90.00-100.00. Robinson Ransbottom Pottery; Chef with bowl of (?) Eggs; Mark: "R.R.P.Co USA Roseville O 411". $32.00-35.00.

Roseville; Clematis; Mark: "Roseville USA 3●8"". $160.00-175.00. Royalware; Bear with Cookie; Mark: "Royalware". $32.00-36.00.

Shawnee; Farmer Pig; Mark: "USA". $55.00-60.00. Shawnee; Farmer Pig with Tulips; Mark: "USA". $70.00-75.00.

Shawnee; Winnie Pig, Blue Collar; Mark: "Patented Winnie USA".
$70.00-75.00.   Shawnee; Farmer Pig, Pink Flowers; Mark: "USA". $75.00-78.00.

Shawnee; Puss 'n Boots; Mark: "Patented Puss 'n' Boots USA".
$70.00-75.00.   Shawnee; Muggsy; Mark: "Patented Muggsy USA". $78.00-85.00.

Shawnee; Dutch Boy; Mark: "USA". $60.00-65.00.   Shawnee; Dutch Girl; Mark: "USA". $60.00-65.00.

Shawnee; Basket of Fruit; Mark: "Shawnee USA 84". $55.00-60.00.   Shawnee; Hexagon Jar; Mark: "USA". $18.00-25.00.

Shawnee; Winnie Pig, Green Collar; Mark: "USA". $70.00-75.00. Shawnee; Farmer Pig, With Clover Leaves; Mark: "USA". $75.00-78.00.

Shawnee; Clown, with Ball and Seal balancing Ball; Mark: "Shawnee USA 12". $90.00-98.00. Shawnee; Ear of Corn; Mark: "Shawnee USA 66". $75.00-85.00.

Shawnee; Winnie Pig, Bank-Cookie Jar; Mark: "Patented Winnie Shawnee USA 61". $115.00-130.00.   Shawnee; Smiley Pig, Bank-Cookie Jar; Mark: "Patented Smiley 60 Shawnee USA". $115.00-130.00.

Shawnee; Winking Owl; Mark: "USA". $78.00-85.00.   Shawnee; Pink Elephant; Mark: "60 Shawnee USA". $42.00-50.00.

Shawnee; Sailor; cold paint; Mark: "USA". $32.00-35.00.   Shawnee; Hexagon with Baker and Gingerbread Boy; Mark: "USA". $45.00-50.00.

Shawnee; Dutch Boy; cold paint trim; yellow pants; Mark: "USA". $25.00-28.00.   Shawnee; Dutch Girl; cold paint trim; yellow skirt; Mark: "USA". $25.00-28.00.

Shawnee; Winnie Pig; coral collar; Mark: "Patented Winnie USA".
$70.00-75.00. Shawnee; Sitting Elephant; cold paint trim; Mark: "USA".
$35.00-38.00.

Shawnee; Dutch Boy; blue pants; cold paint trim; Mark: "USA".
$25.00-28.00. Shawnee; Dutch Girl; blue skirt; cold paint trim; Mark: "USA".
$25.00-28.00.

Shawnee; Cooky, Blonde Haired Dutch Girl; gold trim; "Cooky" is written on her shoulder. Unmarked. $125.00-130.00. Shawnee; Light Brown Haired Dutch Boy; gold trim; "Happy" is written below his pocket. Mark: "USA". $115.00-125.00.

Shawnee; Lucky Elephant; gold trim; "Lucky" is written across his chest. Mark: "USA". $130.00-150.00. Shawnee; Winking Owl; gold trim; Mark: "USA". $125.00-140.00.

Shawnee; Winnie Pig; gold trim; Mark: 'USA". $110.00-125.00.   Shawnee: Smiley Pig; gold trim; "Smiley" is written across his stomach. Mark: "USA". $110.00-125.00.

Shawnee; Puss 'n Boots; flowers and gold trim; Mark: "Patented Puss 'n Boots USA". $115.00-125.00.   Shawnee: Muggsy; flowers and gold trim; Mark: "USA". $125.00-135.00.

Shawnee: Clown with Ball and Seal; gold trim; Mark: "Shawnee USA 12". $140.00-150.00. Shawnee; Sailor; flowers and gold trim; "G O B" is printed on right side by arm. Mark: "USA". $145.00-160.00.

Shawnee: Winnie Pig; gold trim; Mark: "USA". $110.00-125.00. Shawnee; Smiley Pig; gold trim; "Smiley" is written across his stomach. Mark: "USA". $110.00-125.00.

Shawnee; Dutch Boy: white pants; cold paint trim; Mark: "USA". $20.00-25.00. Shawnee; Dutch Boy; blue scarf, flowers and gold trim; "Happy" is written in gold across stomach. Mark: "USA". $115.00-125.00.

Shawnee: Small Dutch Girl; Mark: "Great Northern USA 1026". $120.00-130.00. Sierra Vista; House; Mark: "Sierra Vista 53 California". $38.00-45.00.

Sierra Vista; Stagecoach; Mark: "Sierra Vista Ceramics Pasadena Calif USA 56". $65.00-70.00. Sierra Vista; Train; Mark: "Sierra Vista California". $40.00-45.00.

Sierra Vista; Treasure Chest; Mark: "Sierra Vista Calif 50". $25.00-30.00. Sierra Vista; Humpty Dumpty; Mark: "Sierra Vista Ceramics 57 Pasadena Calif". $32.00-38.00.

Sierra Vista; Old Fashioned Telephone; Mark: "Pat. 44859 Sierra Vista Ceramics Pasadena Calif. USA". $30.00-35.00.   Sierra Vista; Clown Head; Mark: "Sierra Vista California USA". $26.00-30.00.

Sierra Vista; Rooster; Mark: "Sierra Vista California". $35.00-38.00.   Sierra Vista; Square Jar with Rooster; Mark: "Sierra Vista Calif". $22.00-25.00.

Stanfordware; Ear of Corn; Mark: "512 Stanfordware". $65.00-70.00.   Sunshine Biscuits; Pasteboard-type can with metal bottom, lid and bail; Mark: "Sunshine Biscuits Inc. New York, N.Y. Make in USA" $20.00-24.00.

Terrence Ceramics; Boy Pig; Mark: "Smiley Terrence Ceramics". $30.00-35.00.   Treasure Craft; Mouse; Mark: "Treasure Craft USA". $30.00-35.00.

Treasure Craft; Baseball Boy; Mark: "Treasure Craft Made in USA". $25.00-30.00. Treasure Craft; Monk; Mark: "Treasure Craft USA". $28.00-32.00.

Twin Winton; Sailor Mouse; Mark: "Twin Winton San Juan Calif USA". $25.00-30.00. Twin Winton; Collegiate Owl; Mark: "Twin Winton Calif USA". $25.00-30.00.

Twin Winton; Squirrel with Cookie; Mark: "Twin Winton". $25.00-30.00. Twin Winton; Monk; Mark: "Twin Winton San Juan California USA". $35.00-38.00.

Twin Winton; Gold Buddha; Mark: "Twin Winton Santa Monica Calif". $60.00-70.00. Twin Winton; Bear on Stump; Unmarked. $22.00-28.00.

Twin Winton; Bear; Mark : "Twin Winton Calif USA". $32.00-36.00.   Twin Winton; Elephant; Mark: "Twin Winton 60 Made in USA". $25.00-28.00.

Twin Winton; Walrus; Mark: "Twin Winton USA California". $32.00-38.00. Twin Winton; Turtle; Mark: "Twin Winton". $25.00-30.00.

Twin Winton; Elf Bakery Tree Stump; Mark: "Twin Winton Calif USA". $28.00-32.00. Twin Winton; Noah's Ark; Mark: "Twin Winton Calif USA". $25.00-30.00.

Twin Winton; Pig; Mark: "Twin Winton". $30.00-35.00. Twin Winton; Lamb; Unmarked. $28.00-32.00.

Twin Winton; Cow; Mark: "Twin Winton Calif. USA". $35.00-38.00.   Twin Winton; Bull; Unmarked. $22.00-28.00.

Twin Winton; Sitting Horse; Mark: "Twin Winton Made in Calif USA." $30.00-35.00. Twin Winton; Dutch Girl; Mark: "Twin Winton USA". $32.00-38.00.

Twin Winton; Poodle behind Counter; Mark: "Twin Winton Calif USA". $25.00-30.00. Warner Bros.; Porkey Pig; Mark: "1975 Warner Bros". $45.00-50.00.

Watts Pottery; Goodies; Mark: "72 USA Ovenware". $60.00-68.00. Walt Disney Productions; Mickey Mouse Clock; Mark: "Walt Disney Productions". $50.00-60.00.

Walt Disney Productions; Mickey Mouse; Mark: "Patented Turnabout 4 in 1 Mickey and Minnie Walt Disney". $90.00-100.00.   Walt Disney Productions; Minnie Mouse; Reverse side of Mickey.

Walt Disney Productions; Donald Duck; Mark; "Donald Duck & Jose Carioca from the Three Caballeros Walt Disney USA". $95.00-105.00.   Walt Disney Productions; Jose Carioca; Reverse side of Donald Duck.

Walt Disney Productions; Pluto; Mark: "Dumbo-Pluto USA 23 L Walt Disney". $110.00-115.00.   Walt Disney Productions; Dumbo; Reverse side of Pluto.

Walt Disney Productions; Dumbo; Side #1 Mark: "Patented Turnabout 4 in 1 Dumbo Walt Disney". $68.00-75.00.   Walt Disney Productions; Dumbo; Reverse side of #1.

Walt Disney Productions; Thumper; Mark: "Reg U.S. Pat. Off Celebrate Made in USA"; "Walt Disney Productions". $70.00-75.00.   Walt Disney Productions; Alice in Wonderland; Mark: "Alice in Wonderland Walt Disney Prod". $50.00-55.00.

Walt Disney Productions; Donald Duck; Mark: "Reg U.S. Pat. Off Celebrate Made in USA"; "Walt Disney Productions". $90.00-100.00.   Walt Disney Productions; Mickey Mouse; Mark: "Mickey Mouse Walt Disney Prod". $60.00-65.00.

Walt Disney Productions; Donald Duck with Pumpkin; Mark: "Walt Disney Productions 805". $55.00-60.00.   Walt Disney Productions; Mickey Mouse with Drum; Mark; "Walt Disney Productions 864". $55.00-60.00.

Walt Disney Productions; Donald Duck and Nephew; Mark: "Donald Duck Walt Disney Prod". $55.00-60.00.   Walt Disney Productions; Donald Duck and Nephew; Mark: "Donald Duck Walt Disney Prod". $55.00-60.00.

Walt Disney Productions; Mickey on Birthday Cake; Mark: "Walt Disney Productions". $85.00-90.00. Walt Disney Productions; Snow White; Mark: "Walt Disney Productions". $50.00-60.00.

Walt Disney Productions; Winnie the Pooh; Mark: "Walt Disney Productions". $85.00-90.00. Walt Disney Productions; Tigger; Mark: "Walt Disney Productions". $85.00-90.00.

Walt Disney Productions; Donald Duck; Mark: "Donald Duck Walt Disney Productions". $50.00-55.00.   Unknown; Clear Pink; Unmarked. $30.00-35.00.

Unknown; Dads Cookies; This is the largest cookie jar we have. I have seen it in a smaller size which is still big, but the lettering is on the bottom of jar instead of front. Mark: "Property of Dads Cookie Co.". $110.00-125.00.

Pottery Guild; Elsie the Cow; Unmarked. $70.00-75.00. Unknown; Girl Pig with Shamrock indentions; (Possibly made by American Bisque); Unmarked. $50.00-55.00.

Regal China; Goldilocks;; Mark: "405 "Goldilocks" Pat. Pending". $115.00-125.00. Regal China; Barn; Unmarked. $75.00-90.00.

Unknown

Unknown; Black Chef Head; Unmarked. $25.00-30.00.   Unknown; Yellow Chef Head; Unmarked. $18.00-22.00.

Sierra Vista; Clown Bust; Unmarked. $30.00-35.00.   Unknown; Cookie Cop; Unmarked. $50.00-55.00.

Unknown; Duck; Mark: "USA 10". $50.00-55.00.   Unknown; Barefoot Boy; (Possibly made for Hull); Unmarked. $175.00-190.00.

Pottery Guild; Little Red Riding Hood; Unmarked. $78.00-85.00.   Unknown; Rabbit; Mark: "Patent Pending". $30.00-35.00.

Unknown; Rabbit with Carrot; brown stoneware; Unmarked.
$15.00-18.00. Unknown; Rabbit with Carrot; aqua stoneware; Unmarked.
$15.00-18.00.

Unknown; Little Hen; Unmarked. $50.00-60.00. Unknown; Scarecrow;
Unmarked. $35.00-38.00.

California Original; Sheriff with Hole in Hat; Unmarked. $35.00-38.00. California Originals; Indian with Lollipop; Unmarked. $35.00-38.00.

California Original; Gum Ball Machine; Mark: "890 USA". $25.00-30.00. Ludowici Celadon; Fluffy Cat; Mark: "Fluffy USA". $45.00-48.00.

Unknown; Dog in Basket; Mark: "Patent Pending". $30.00-35.00.   Unknown;
Cat in Basket; Mark: "Patent Pending". $30.00-35.00.

Unknown; Rabbit in Basket; Mark: "Patent Pending". $30.00-35.00.   Unknown;
Black Jar; yellow indented flowers; Unmarked. $15.00-18.00.

Unknown; Maroon Jar with Girls and Mountain scene; Unmarked. $15.00-18.00. Unknown; Red Riding Hood; Unmarked. $35.00-38.00.

Maurice of California; Clown; Unmarked. $55.00-60.00.

Unknown; Baby Boy Duck; Mark: "Patent App. USA". $30.00-35.00.   Unknown;
Baby Girl Duck; Unmarked. $25.00-30.00.

Unknown; Full Figure Clown; Unmarked. $35.00-38.00.   Unknown; Toll House
Cookies; Original Nestle Toll House Cookie Recipe on back of Jar; Unmarked.
$45.00-50.00.

Regal China; Chef with Salad Bowl; Mark: "54-192". $60.00-75.00. Unknown; Angel Cook; Unmarked. $60.00-75.00.

Unknown; Doll and Blocks on Stoneware; Unmarked. $25.00-30.00. Unknown; Aqua Stoneware with Fruit; Unmarked. $15.00-18.00.

Unknown; Merry-Go-Round; Mark: "S4 USA". $25.00-30.00.   Unknown; Bucket Shape; Mark: "Ovenproof USA" $15.00-18.00.

Unknown; Gingerbread Boy, Girl on Reverse; Unmarked. $20.00-25.00. Unknown; Brown Bear; Unmarked. $25.00-30.00.

Unknown; Animal Cookies; Brown Stoneware; Unmarked. $18.00-25.00.
Unknown; Animal Cookies; Blue Stoneware; Unmarked. $15.00-20.00.

Unknown; Cookie Corral; Unmarked. $25.00-30.00.   Unknown; Cowboy with
Lasso; Unmarked. $25.00-30.00.

Unknown

Ludowici Celadon; Girl Bear; Mark: "Patent Applied Turn About The 4 in 1 USA". $38.00-42.00. Ludowici Celadon; Boy Bear, Reverse side of Girl.

Pottery Guild; Dutch Boy; Unmarked. $52.00-58.00.   Pottery Guild; Dutch Girl; Unmarked. $52.00-58.00.

Unknown; Cow Jumped over the Moon; brown jar; Unmarked. $32.00-38.00.
Unknown; Cow Jumped over the Moon; tan jar; Unmarked. $32.00-38.00.

Unknown; Merry-Go-Round; Unmarked. $25.00-28.00.   Unknown; Black Pitcher
with Raspberries; Unmarked. $15.00-18.00.

Unknown

Unknown; Soldier; Unmarked. $35.00-40.00. Unknown; Air Corp or Marine; Unmarked. $35.00-40.00.

Unknown; Chef; Unmarked. $35.00-40.00. Unknown; Campbell Kids; Unmarked. $38.00-42.00.

Unknown; Tan Jar with 3 Blind Mice; Unmarked. $18.00-22.00.   Unknown; Aqua Jar with 3 Blind Mice; Unmarked. $18.00-22.00.

Unknown; Cookies with Pretzel on Lid; Mark: "USA". $20.00-25.00.   Unknown; Owl: Unmarked. $22.00-25.00.

Unknown; Blue Beanpot-Type with White Flowers; Mark: "Made in USA".
$20.00-25.00.   Unknown; Strawberry with Bloom on Lid; Mark: "Sears exclusively USA Patent Pending". $25.00-30.00.

Doranne of California; Fancy Cat; Unmarked. $30.00-35.00.   California
Originals; Frog; Mark: "2645 USA". $32.00-38.00.

Unknown; Pig Head; Unmarked. $20.00-25.00.   Regal China; Cat with Flowers
and Gold Trim; This jar seems as though it was copied after the Shawnee Puss
'n Boots, except this one has a fish on the hat instead of a bird; the bow is
different and the nose has a pinched look. The inside of the head is the only
part that isn't glazed. Unmarked. $60.00-65.00.

Unknown; Panda; Unmarked. $35.00-38.00.   American Bisque; Indian Lady; Un-
marked. $60.00-65.00.

Unknown

Unknown; Bear; Unmarked. $25.00-28.00.   House of Webster; Little School House; Unmarked. $38.00-42.00.

Unknown; Baseball Boy with Bat; Mark: "875 USA". $25.00-30.00.   Unknown; Brown Bagger; Unmarked. $25.00-28.00.

California Original; Unknown; Santa Claus; Mark: "871".
$35.00-50.00. Unknown; Elephant with Ric-Rac Trim; Mark: "W-) '58".
$20.00-25.00.

California Original; Little Red Riding Hood; Mark: "320".
$32.00-36.00. Unknown; Old Fashioned Radio; Unmarked. $30.00-35.00.

Unknown; Clown; Mark: "Calif 483 USA". $25.00-30.00.   Unknown; Tug Boat;
Mark: "California". $45.00-50.00.

Unknown; Standing Elephant; Mark: "USA". $25.00-28.00.   Unknown; Mam-
my; Unmarked. $100.00-115.00.

Price Guide

Page 5

Granny $150.00-165.00
Black Little Old Lady $350.00-500.00
Hobby Horse $125.00-140.00
Hippo..................................... $130.00-150.00

Page 6

Train $115.00-125.00
Three Bears............................ $100.00-115.00
Humpty Dumpty "663" $135.00-150.00
Humpty Dumpty "707" $150.00-175.00

Page 7

Clock $68.00-72.00
Jack-in-Box $180.00-210.00
Money Sack "558" $60.00-65.00
Money Sack "588" $70.00-75.00

Page 8

Little Miss Muffet "662" $175.00-190.00
Little Miss Muffet "705" $190.00-210.00
Mother Goose $200.00-250.00
Little Bo-Peep $190.00-225.00

Page 9

Daisy $75.00-90.00
Pineapple $70.00-85.00
Paddys Pig; cream $15.00-18.00
Paddys Pig; blue $15.00-18.00

Page 10

Dutch Girl............................... $35.00-40.00
Dutch Boy $45.00-55.00
Ring Cookies........................... $10.00-15.00
Pig.. $30.00-36.00

Page 11

Cow $30.00-36.00
Lamb $38.00-40.00
Apple...................................... $15.00-18.00
Clown $30.00-35.00

Page 12

Dutch Girl............................... $50.00-60.00
Candy Baby $35.00-38.00
Boy Baby Elephant $50.00-58.00
Girl Baby Elephant.................. $50.00-58.00

Page 13

Martha and George.................. $15.00-20.00
Rabbit in Hat $45.00-60.00
Buck Lamb $50.00-65.00
Girl Lamb $40.00-50.00

Page 14

Sitting Horse $150.00-175.00
Donkey w/Milk Wagon............... $65.00-70.00
Granny $45.00-50.00
Sandman Cookies.................... $55.00-60.00

Page 15

Churn boy............................... $110.00-125.00
Umbrella Kids.......................... $80.00-100.00
Chef $35.00-40.00
Merry-Go-Round $28.00-35.00

Page 16

Cat on Beehive $35.00-42.00
Kittens w/Ball of Yarn $35.00-42.00
Ring for Cookies $25.00-28.00
Black Heating Stove.................. $18.00-22.00

Page 17

Blackboard Clown $100.00-125.00
Blackboard Bum.................... $100.00-125.00
Blackboard School Boy $110.00-130.00
Blackboard Little Girl $110.00-130.00

Page 18

Churn $12.00-15.00
Clock $28.00-32.00
Cheerleaders........................... $90.00-115.00
After School Cookies $28.00-32.00

Page 19

Boy Pig.................................... $45.00-50.00
Lady Pig $45.00-50.00
Baby Pig $115.00-130.00
Pig in the Poke $40.00-50.00

Page 20

Cookie Truck $38.00-42.00
Train $25.00-30.00
Rooster $32.00-35.00
Animal Cookies $20.00-25.00

Page 21

Yarn Doll.................................. $55.00-60.00
Cookie Barrel $10.00-12.00
Sad Iron $40.00-45.00
Majorette $50.00-58.00

Page 22

Recipe Jar............................... $60.00-68.00
Pinecones Coffee Pot $20.00-28.00
Black Coffee Pot $10.00-12.00
Boots...................................... $90.00-100.00

Page 23

Cup of Chocolate $28.00-32.00
Cup and Cookies Coffee Pot...... $20.00-25.00
Puppy in Blue Pot $32.00-36.00
Puppy in Yellow Pot $32.00-36.00

Page 24

Collegiate Owl........................... $35.00-38.00
Wooden Soldier......................... $45.00-50.00
Yellow Chick.............................. $38.00-42.00
White Chick............................... $46.00-55.00

Page 25

Jack in the Box......................... $45.00-50.00
Clown on Stage........................ $40.00-45.00
Bear; eyes open........................ $28.00-32.00
Bear; eyes closed $42.00-48.00

Page 26

Pig.. $50.00-58.00
Cat $45.00-50.00
Clown $45.00-50.00
Chick $45.00-50.00

Page 27

Clown $35.00-38.00
Elephant..$40.00-45.00
Poodle...$55.00-60.00
Cat $35.00-38.00

Page 28

Snacks $12.00-15.00
Bear w/Cookie......................................$42.00-48.00
Pig $55.00-60.00
Rooster $32.00-38.00

Page 29

Farmer Pig $60.00-65.00
Seal on Igloo $85.00-90.00
Spaceship $80.00-95.00
Rabbit $50.00-65.00

Page 30

Lion $35.00-38.00
Mammy $500.00-600.00
Lantern..$50.00-55.00
Brown Cow...$90.00-125.00

Page 31

Little Boy Blue $175.00-200.00
House..$48.00-56.00
Humpty Dumpty w/Beanie $125.00-150.00
Humpty Dumpty w/Cowboy Hat ...$85.00-95.00

Page 32

Panda Bear $125.00-140.00
Praying Girl $50.00-55.00
Tulips..$28.00-32.00
Hen on Nest $35.00-38.00

Page 33

Treasure Chest.....................................$90.00-115.00
Chick on Nest.......................................$125.00-140.00
Granny...$90.00-110.00
Old Woman's Shoe $85.00-100.00

Page 34

Clock $100.00-115.00
Little Girl...$135.00-150.00
Grey Bunny $100.00-125.00
White Bunny $90.00-115.00

Page 35

Teddy Bear; feet apart..........................$78.00-95.00
Teddy Bear; feet together......................$60.00-75.00
Davy Crockett $160.00-185.00
Puppy Police $125.00-140.00

Page 36

Three Bears $40.00-55.00
Covered Wagon $240.00-275.00
Donkey w/Cart $130.00-145.00
Formal Pig..$85.00-100.00

Page 37

Happy Squirrel......................................$95.00-115.00
Squirrel on Log.....................................$60.00-75.00
Peter Peter Pumpkin Eater $125.00-150.00
Cinderella's Pumpkin.............$115.00-140.00

Page 38

Clown $115.00-125.00
Circus Horse $200.00-250.00
Elephant; blue coat $125.00-150.00
Elephant; yellow coat $125.00-150.00

Page 39

Little Red Riding Hood $175.00-200.00
Dog w/ Basket......................................$65.00-80.00
Pelican $45.00-50.00
Brown Bear $35.00-45.00

Page 40

Rabbit..$20.00-25.00
Elfs School House.................................$40.00-50.00
Ernie..$55.00-60.00
Cookie Monster.....................................$42.00-48.00

Page 41

Count $75.00-100.00
Smokey Bear $35.00-40.00
Cookie Garage $42.00-45.00
Boy's Head...$50.00-65.00

Page 42

Soldier...$55.00-60.00
Round House $42.00-48.00
French Chef $48.00-55.00
Cookie Safe $25.00-30.00

Page 43

Sack of cookies.....................................$28.00-32.00
Milk Can $32.00-38.00
Cookie King...$50.00-55.00
Clown $35.00-40.00

Page 44

Cow Jumped over the Moon $90.00-110.00
Shoe..$20.00-25.00
Mother Goose $70.00-75.00
Hen w/Basket of Eggs...............$30.00-35.00

Page 45

Duck w/Corn $30.00-35.00
Fire Plug..$32.00-38.00
Cow w/Milk Can $30.00-35.00
Aunt Jemima $185.00-195.00

Page 46

Brown & Beige $35.00-40.00
Green & Grey Concave...........$25.00-28.00
Black Barrel w/Ears................................$30.00-35.00
Pink Dove...$40.00-45.00

Page 47

Green dove $40.00-45.00
Blue Dove $40.00-45.00
Brown Chicken......................................$30.00-35.00
Brown & Green Chicken $30.00-35.00

Page 48

Windmill; red $35.00-38.00
Windmill; blue.......................................$40.00-50.00
Rooster $35.00-40.00
White and Gold $58.00-62.00

Page 49

Poppy $70.00-80.00
Autumn Leaf...........................$120.00-130.00
Yogi Bear.................................$125.00-150.00
Casper $300.00-350.00

Page 50

Big Apple...................................$25.00-28.00
Duck..$45.00-55.00
Little Red Riding Hood "967"..$115.00-140.00
Little Red Riding Hood $110.00-125.00

Page 51

Little Red Riding Hood "967"..$110.00-125.00
Little Red Riding Hood "967"..$115.00-140.00
Little Red Riding Hood $100.00-110.00
Daisy $25.00-28.00

Page 52

Cookies and Cookie Cutters $35.00-38.00
Cookies w/Nut on Lid $20.00-25.00
Apple and Apple Blossoms $15.00-18.00
Humpty Dumpty $45.00-55.00

Page 53

Brown w/Flowers and Dots $25.00-30.00
Kittens in Shoe...........................$40.00-50.00
Love Me Puppy $18.00-22.00
Love Me Puppy, gloss finish......$15.00-18.00

Page 54

Rabbit...$38.00-42.00
Bear beating Drum.....................$25.00-28.00
Hen w/Chicks $50.00-60.00
Turkey w/Little Turkey on Back ..$80.00-95.00

Page 55

Dark Indian.............................$175.00-200.00
Light Indian $180.00-210.00
Tepee $150.00-170.00
Honey Bear $68.00-72.00

Page 56

Log Cabin..................................$55.00-65.00
Davy Crockett $350.00-375.00
Circus Horse $90.00-100.00
Barnum's Animals $90.00-100.00

Page 57

Clown Bust.................................$40.00-50.00
Animal Crackers........................$30.00-35.00
Sad Clown..................................$50.00-65.00
Little Clown $60.00-65.00

Page 58

Dutch Girl $55.00-60.00
Dutch Boy $30.00-32.00
Windmill $60.00-75.00
Dutch Treat Barn.......................$25.00-28.00

Page 59

Fat Pig.......................................$40.00-45.00
Ear of Corn.............................$100.00-125.00
Betsy Baker...............................$80.00-90.00
Bobby Baker $30.00-35.00

Page 60

Black Cookstove $35.00-40.00
White Cookstove $25.00-32.00
Chef Head.................................$60.00-80.00
Mammy w/Cauliflower $800.00-1,000.00

Page 61

Old Strawberry $32.00-35.00
Pineapple $35.00-40.00
Orange $55.00-60.00
Lemon $40.00-45.00

Page 62

Red Apple $25.00-28.00
Bunch of Bananas.....................$70.00-85.00
Christmas Tree......................$300.00-350.00
Pinecones on Basketweave.......$30.00-35.00

Page 63

Raggedy Ann $45.00-50.00
Fireplace $70.00-80.00
Jack-O-Lantern $325.00-375.00
Black Cat...................................$80.00-90.00

Page 64

Polar Bear $65.00-68.00
Polar Bear "McCoy" $40.00-45.00
Brown Bear $80.00-90.00
Hamms Bear $90.00-115.00

Page 65

Snow Bear $55.00-60.00
Upside Down Bear $32.00-38.00
Kissing Penguins $70.00-80.00
White Pel-guins $60.00-70.00

Page 66

Green Pel-guin $90.00-100.00
Yellow Pel-guin.........................$85.00-90.00
Chiffonier...................................$58.00-65.00
Rooster $35.00-40.00

Page 67

Frontier Family $50.00-60.00
Frontier Family ....Reverse side
Cookie Safe $35.00-40.00
Cookie Bank..............................$80.00-90.00

Page 68

Cookie House $80.00-90.00
Churn $15.00-18.00
Black Train Engine $100.00-125.00
Caboose................................$90.00-100.00

Page 69

Cookie Wagon...........................$85.00-90.00
Touring Car $75.00-80.00
Hobby Horse; white...................$60.00-65.00
Hobby Horse; brown $70.00-75.00

Page 70

Mushrooms on Stump...............$35.00-42.00
Rabbit on Stump $35.00-42.00
Squirrel on Log..........................$20.00-25.00
Cookie Boy $80.00-90.00

163

Page 71

Monkey on Stump	$35.00-42.00
Cookie boy	$80.00-85.00
Burlap Bag	$18.00-22.00
Burlap Bag w/Redbird	$28.00-32.00

Page 72

Wren House; pink bird	$72.00-80.00
Wren House; brown bird	$65.00-70.00
Pears on Basketweave	$30.00-35.00
Yellow Pear	$70.00-75.00

Page 73

Forbidden Fruit	$45.00-50.00
New Strawberry	$30.00-35.00
Apples on Basketweave	$30.00-35.00
Yellow Apple	$35.00-40.00

Page 74

Mouse on Clock	$28.00-32.00
Lollipops	$30.00-35.00
Yellow Mouse	$18.00-24.00
Grandfather Clock	$65.00-70.00

Page 75

Black Lantern	$42.00-48.00
Fortune Cookies	$28.00-32.00
Granny	$50.00-55.00
Mammy	$100.00-110.00

Page 76

W. C. Fields	$100.00-125.00
Lamb on Basketweave	$38.00-42.00
Monk	$25.00-28.00
Hobnail	$20.00-25.00

Page 77

Cylinder w/Fruit	$18.00-22.00
Cylinder w/Vegetables	$18.00-22.00
Yellow Pepper	$15.00-18.00
Green Pepper	$15.00-18.00

Page 78

Wedding Jar	$55.00-60.00
Coffee Grinder	$30.00-35.00
Bugs Bunny	$45.00-48.00
Popeye	$55.00-60.00

Page 79

Yosemite Sam	$45.00-48.00
Bronze Milk Can	$25.00-28.00
Brown Cat	$40.00-45.00
Cat on Basketweave	$38.00-40.00

Page 80

Three Little Kittens; Maroon	$50.00-55.00
Three Little Kittens; Yellow	$50.00-55.00
Three Little Kittens; Green	$50.00-55.00
Two Kittens in Basket	$200.00-225.00

Page 81

Basket of Fruit	$50.00-60.00
Picnic Basket	$45.00-55.00
Cookie Pot	$35.00-38.00
Coffee Mug	$30.00-35.00

Page 82

Gaytime Pitcher; small	$30.00-35.00
Gaytime Pitcher, grown	$30.00-35.00
Yellow Rooster	$60.00-68.00
Hen on Nest	$55.00-60.00

Page 83

Grey Rooster	$65.00-70.00
Basket of Eggs	$22.00-25.00
Duck w/Leaf	$65.00-80.00
Turkey	$120.00-135.00

Page 84

Tan Basketweave	$18.00-22.00
Brown Basketweave	$22.00-25.00
Friendship 7	$80.00-90.00
World Globe	$115.00-125.00

Page 85

Astronauts	$150.00-165.00
Apollo	$375.00-450.00
Dog in Basket	$52.00-58.00
Snoopy on Dog House	$150.00-175.00

Page 86

Thinking Puppy	$20.00-25.00
Puppy Holding Sign	$48.00-52.00
Rocking Chair Dalmations	$180.00-200.00
Mac Dog	$55.00-60.00

Page 87

Sack of Cookies	$42.00-48.00
Chipmunk	$85.00-100.00
Black Pot Bellied Stove	$35.00-40.00
White Pot Bellied Stove	$38.00-42.00

Page 88

Kangaroo	$215.00-225.00
Blue Kangaroo	$100.00-115.00
Elephant	$100.00-125.00
Drum	$40.00-50.00

Page 89

Mother Goose; brown	$85.00-90.00
Mother Goose; white	$80.00-88.00
Wishing Well	$35.00-40.00
Square	$15.00-20.00

Page 90

Oaken Bucket	$12.00-15.00
Double Headed Duck	$42.00-48.00
Asparagus	$25.00-30.00
Basket of Potatoes	$28.00-32.00

Page 91

White Cylinder w/Chef	$22.00-28.00
White Cylinder w/Apple	$18.00-22.00
Nabisco Jar	$55.00-65.00
White Cylinder w/Wheat	$20.00-25.00

Page 92

Mr. & Mrs. Owl	$78.00-85.00
Brown Owl	$22.00-25.00
Woodsy Owl	$100.00-115.00
Hocus Rabbit	$25.00-30.00

Page 93

Rabbit; cream............................$30.00-35.00
Timmy Tortoise...........................$35.00-38.00
Mary, Mary $40.00-50.00
Little Bo-Peep $40.00-50.00

Page 94

Humpty Dumpty $40.00-50.00
Little Miss Muffet $40.00-50.00
Brown Barrel $20.00-25.00
Black Barrel...............................$18.00-22.00

Page 95

Tureen......................................$35.00-40.00
Tomato $40.00-50.00
Gingerbread Man $55.00-60.00
Kissin' Don't Last Cookin' Do.....$25.00-30.00

Page 96

Small Brown Cookie Barrel........$15.00-20.00
Large Brown Cookie Barrel.......$12.00-15.00
Clown in Yellow Barrel $55.00-60.00
Clown in Blue Barrel $55.00-60.00

Page 97

Clown in Green Barrel................$55.00-60.00
Pirates Chest $70.00-75.00
White w/Gold Trim......................$35.00-40.00
Pitcher w/Blue Willow Decor $35.00-40.00

Page 98

Clyde Dog $45.00-50.00
Animal Cracker Clown $38.00-42.00
Basket of Strawberries.............$28.00-32.00
Dog in Dog House....................$50.00-55.00

Page 99

Cookie Box.................................$65.00-68.00
Liberty Bell $38.00-42.00
Football $75.00-90.00
Baseball $75.00-90.00

Page 100

Basket of Tomatoes $25.00-28.00
Koala Bear $35.00-40.00
Mammy $180.00-200.00
Chef $150.00-180.00

Page 101

Bo-Peep....................................$50.00-55.00
Tomato $20.00-25.00
Clown $45.00-50.00
Southern Belle $54.00-60.00

Page 102

Chef $450.00-525.00
Mammy $525.00-600.00
Albert Apple $60.00-68.00
Stella Strawberry......................$68.00-72.00

Page 103

Derby Dan..................................$50.00-55.00
Pillsbury Doughboy $50.00-60.00
Bear $40.00-45.00
Squirrel on Stump $30.00-38.00

Page 104

Rose..$45.00-55.00
Drum w/Girl, Boy and Dog $35.00-40.00
Raggedy Andy $50.00-60.00
Raggedy Ann $50.00-60.00

Page 105

The Bandit.................................$50.00-55.00
Mouse Mobile............................$38.00-42.00
Squirrel on Pinecone.................$30.00-35.00
Clown $60.00-75.00

Page 106

Lamb Head $30.00-35.00
Cat Head...................................$30.00-36.00
Pig..$35.00-40.00
Rooster $40.00-45.00

Page 107

Black Ball Shape.......................$30.00-35.00
Aqua w/Dutch People $55.00-60.00
Yellow Baker $55.00-60.00
Yellow Dutch Girl......................$58.00-65.00

Page 108

Blue Baker $55.00-60.00
Blue Dutch girl...........................$60.00-65.00
Beige Baker $55.00-60.00
Beige Dutch Girl........................$60.00-65.00

Page 109

Bob White $70.00-80.00
Pineapple $40.00-45.00
Beige Monk $55.00-60.00
Blue Monk $65.00-70.00

Page 110

Quaker Oats..........................$115.00-125.00
Davy Crockett Head...............$125.00-150.00
Oscar $45.00-50.00
Girl Head...................................$40.00-50.00

Page 111

Brownie $50.00-60.00
Firechief....................................$50.00-60.00
Captain......................................$50.00-60.00
Preacher $50.00-60.00

Page 112

World War II Soldier $60.00-75.00
World War I Soldier $65.00-70.00
Brown Rooster $35.00-40.00
Cream Colored w/Aqua Rings ...$30.00-35.00

Page 113

Sheriff Pig; yellow hat................$35.00-40.00
Sheriff Pig; grey hat...................$35.00-40.00
Peter, Peter, Pumpkin Eater.....$90.00-110.00
Cow Jumped over the Moon $68.00-72.00

Page 114

Jocko..$80.00-100.00
Wise Bird...................................$30.00-35.00
Snowman $135.00-150.00
Chef w/ bowl $38.00-42.00

Page 115

Clematis $190.00-210.00
Bear w/Cookie...........................$32.00-36.00
Farmer Pig $90.00-100.00
Farmer Pig w/Tulips $105.00-120.00

Page 116

Winnie Pig $110.00-120.00
Farmer Pig................................$110.00-120.00
Puss 'n Boots $115.00-125.00
Muggsy $125.00-135.00

Page 117

Dutch Boy................................$90.00-110.00
Dutch girl $90.00-110.00
Basket of Fruit.........................$65.00-70.00
Hexagon Jar.............................$20.00-28.00

Page 118

Winnie Pig $110.00-120.00
Farmer Pig................................$110.00-120.00
Clown $125.00-150.00
Ear of Corn...............................$90.00-100.00

Page 119

Winnie Pig...............................$150.00-170.00
Smiley Pig $150.00-170.00
Winking Owl.............................$110.00-115.00
Pink Elephant...........................$60.00-65.00

Page 120

Sailor.......................................$50.00-75.00
Hexagon...................................$55.00-62.00
Dutch Boy $30.00-35.00
Dutch Girl $30.00-35.00

Page 121

Winnie Pig $110.00-115.00
Sitting Elephant........................$50.00-55.00
Dutch Boy $30.00-35.00
Dutch Girl $30.00-35.00

Page 122

Dutch Girl $140.00-150.00
Dutch Boy $130.00-140.00
Lucky Elephant $200.00-250.00
Winking Owl $160.00-175.00

Page 123

Winnie Pig................................$145.00-150.00
Smiley Pig $145.00-150.00
Puss 'n Boots $220.00-230.00
Muggsy $225.00-240.00

Page 124

Clown $220.00-250.00
Sailor.......................................$230.00-250.00
Winnie Pig................................$150.00-160.00
Smiley Pig................................$145.00-160.00

Page 125

Dutch Boy; white pants $30.00-35.00
Dutch Boy; blue scarf............$140.00-150.00
Dutch Girl $150.00-170.00
House.......................................$50.00-55.00

Page 126

Stagecoach $75.00-80.00
Train...$60.00-70.00
Treasure Chest $32.00-38.00
Humpty Dumpty $50.00-55.00

Page 127

Old Fashioned Telephone $45.00-50.00
Clown Head $26.00-30.00
Rooster $40.00-45.00
Square Jar w/Rooster $28.00-35.00

Page 128

Ear of Corn...............................$80.00-90.00
Sunshine Biscuits.....................$35.00-50.00
Boy Pig.....................................$40.00-50.00
Mouse $38.00-42.00

Page 129

Baseball Boy $50.00-62.00
Monk $35.00-38.00
Sailor Mouse $35.00-40.00
Collegiate Owl...........................$35.00-40.00

Page 130

Squirrel w/Cookie $35.00-40.00
Monk $50.00-60.00
Gold Buddha $90.00-100.00
Bear on Stump $30.00-35.00

Page 131

Bear $35.00-40.00
Elephant....................................$30.00-36.00
Walrus......................................$40.00-50.00
Turtle $30.00-40.00

Page 132

Elf Bakery Tree Stump $40.00-50.00
Noah's Ark................................$35.00-50.00
Pig..$40.00-50.00
Lamb $35.00-40.00

Page 133

Cow $50.00-58.00
Bull $35.00-40.00
Sitting Horse $40.00-50.00
Dutch Girl $48.00-55.00

Page 134

Poodle behind Counter $40.00-50.00
Porkey Pig................................$60.00-75.00
Goodies....................................$70.00-75.00
Mickey Mouse Clock $115.00-125.00

Page 135

Mickey Mouse/Minnie............$115.00-120.00
Donald Duck/Joe Carioca.......$110.00-120.00

Page 136

Pluto/Dumbo...........................$115.00-125.00
Dumbo $100.00-110.00

Page 137

Thumper....................................$70.00-75.00
Alice in Wonderland $60.00-75.00
Donald Duck $140.00-160.00
Mickey Mouse $65.00-80.00

Page 138
Donald Duck $70.00-85.00
Mickey Mouse $75.00-100.00
Donald Duck and Nephew $55.00-60.00
Donald Duck and Nephew $55.00-60.00
Page 139
Mickey on Birthday Cake $125.00-130.00
Snow White...........................$135.00-150.00
Winnie the Pooh.......................$85.00-90.00
Tigger.....................................$85.00-90.00
Page 140
Donald Duck $50.00-55.00
Clear Pink $30.00-35.00
Dad's Cookies $110.00-125.00
Page 141
Elsie the Cow $100.00-125.00
Girl Pig $60.00-70.00
Goldilocks $140.00-170.00
Barn $100.00-125.00
Page 142
Black Chef Head $40.00-50.00
Yellow Chef Head......................$18.00-22.00
Clown Bust...............................$40.00-48.00
Cookie Cop $54.00-60.00
Page 143
Duck..$65.00-70.00
Barefoot Boy $200.00-235.00
Little Red Riding Hood $80.00-90.00
Rabbit......................................$32.00-38.00
Page 144
Rabbit w/Carrot; brown $18.00-25.00
Rabbit w/Carrot; aqua $18.00-25.00
Little Hen.................................$60.00-75.00
Scarecrow $35.00-38.00
Page 145
Sheriff w/Hole in Hat $40.00-50.00
Indian w/Lollipop $40.00-50.00
Gum Ball Machine......................$30.00-38.00
Fluffy Cat..................................$50.00-55.00
Page 146
Dog in Basket............................$35.00-40.00
Cat in Basket.............................$35.00-40.00
Rabbit in Basket.........................$35.00-40.00
Black Jar $15.00-18.00
Page 147
Maroon Jar................................$15.00-18.00
Red Riding Hood.......................$45.00-50.00
Clown $80.00-90.00
Page 148
Baby Boy Duck $30.00-35.00
Baby Girl Duck $25.00-30.00
Clown $40.00-45.00
Toll House Cookies $60.00-75.00

Page 149
Chef w/ Salad Bowl $100.00-125.00
Angel Cook............................$115.00-135.00
Doll and Blocks $40.00-45.00
Aqua Stoneware w/Fruit.............$15.00-18.00
Page 150
Merry-Go-Round $25.00-30.00
Bucket......................................$15.00-18.00
Gingerbread Boy $30.00-40.00
Brown Bear $25.00-30.00
Page 151
Animal Cookies; brown $18.00-25.00
Animal Cookies; blue $15.00-20.00
Cookie Corral $30.00-35.00
Cowboy w/Lasso $30.00-35.00
Page 152
Girl Bear...................................$40.00-50.00
Dutch Boy $55.00-60.00
Dutch Girl $55.00-60.00
Page 153
Cow Jumped over the Moon; brown ..$35.00-45.00
Cow Jumped over the Moon; tan ...$35.00-45.00
Merry-Go-Round $25.00-28.00
Black Pitcher w/Raspberries $15.00-18.00
Page 154
Soldier......................................$40.00-50.00
Air Corp or Marine.....................$40.00-50.00
Chef $40.00-50.00
Campbell Kids $55.00-60.00
Page 155
Tan Jar w/3 Blind Mice $25.00-28.00
Aqua Jar w/3 blind Mice.............$25.00-28.00
Cookies w/ Pretzel on Lid $30.00-38.00
Owl...$22.00-25.00
Page 156
Blue Beanpot-Type $20.00-25.00
Strawberry $40.00-45.00
Fancy Cat..................................$30.00-35.00
Frog..$40.00-45.00
Page 157
Pig..$20.00-25.00
Cat $125.00-140.00
Panda..$45.00-50.00
Indian Lady $60.00-65.00
Page 158
Bear $25.00-28.00
Little School House $38.00-42.00
Baseball Boy $50.00-60.00
Brown Bagger $40.00-50.00
Page 159
Santa Claus $60.00-75.00
Elephant....................................$28.00-32.00
Little Red Riding Hood $50.00-60.00
Old Fashioned Radio $45.00-50.00
Page 160
Clown $40.00-50.00
Tug Boat...................................$70.00-80.00
Standing Elephant......................$25.00-28.00
Mammy $165.00-200.00

Schroeder's Antiques Price Guide

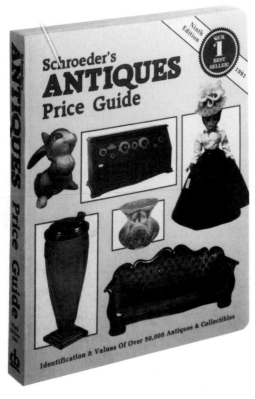

Schroeder's Antiques Price Guide has climbed its way to the top in a field already supplied with several well-established publications! The word is out, *Schroeder's Price Guide* is the best buy at any price. Over 500 categories are covered, with more than 50,000 listings. From ABC Plates to Zsolnay, if it merits the interest of today's collector, you'll find it in Schroeder's. Each subject is represented with histories and background information. In addition, hundreds of sharp original photos are used each year to illustrate not only the rare and the unusual, but the everyday "fun-type" collectibles as well. All new copy and all new illustrations make Schroeder's THE price guide on antiques and collectibles. We have not and will not simply change prices in each new edition.

The writing and researching team is backed by a staff of more than seventy of Collector Books' finest authors, as well as a board of advisors made up of well-known antique authorities and the country's top dealers, all specialists in their fields. Prices are gathered over the entire year previous to publication, then each category is thoroughly checked. Only the best of the lot remains for publication. You'll find the new edition of *Schroeder's Antiques Price Guide* the one to buy for factual information and quality.

No dealer, collector or investor can afford not to own this book. It is available from your favorite bookseller or antiques dealer at the low price of $12.95. If you are unable to find this price guide in your area, it's available from Collector Books, P.O. Box 3009, Paducah, KY 42001 at $12.95 plus $2.00 for postage and handling.